The Instruction Manual for

RECEIVING GOD

Other Books by Jason Shulman

The Instruction Manual for

RECEIVING GOD

JASON SHULMAN

SOUNDS TRUE

Sounds True, Inc.
Boulder, CO 80306

ISBN 978-1-59179-519-3

Printed in the U.S.A.

For Arlene: the seed, tree, and fruit of my life

CONTENTS

ACKNOWLEDGMENTS

The words in this book were first spoken—in a different form—to my students, and it is to them that I first direct my gratitude. Our spiritual lives together, searching for and finding Reality and God, are the truest contents of this book.

I thank my wife, teacher, and companion, Arlene, who came up with the idea for this book.

My thanks also go to people who are no longer with us: Rebbe Nachman of Breslov, Dogen Zenji, Ramakrishna, Ramana Maharshi, and the many others who have been an inspiration to me and have helped me explore all the dark and light places of life. I thank Norman Trager for his steadfast help and enlightening insight, and Terry Horwitz, who has given me first-hand knowledge of the Divine Mother. I am also grateful to the authors of the Prajnaparamita Sutra, the Flower Ornament Scripture, the Zohar, and all the other sacred texts that have proved to be diligent and precise guides to seeing the truth of existence.

My thanks to Nancy Yeilding for her sensitive editing of my text, and to Nancy Pollock, Joan Brady, Alex Gordon-Brander, Tom Schneider, and the Reverend Carol

Bamesberger for their support and efforts to get this text to the public.

My additional thanks go to the staff at Sounds True: Tami Simon, Kelly Notaras, Karen Polaski, Haven Iverson, Beverly Yates, and all the others who are dedicated to an openhearted approach to publishing.

Finally, I thank the rolling hills of New Jersey, the pitch pine forests of Truro, and the wonderful town of Provincetown, Massachusetts, all of which always sound a call to return to my humanity.

INTRODUCTION

There are many books that tell us how to find God. But the truth is that God is not lost or hiding. In fact, it is the actual, continuous, omnipresence of God that is so hard for the human mind to fathom.

We always look in the wrong direction: toward someplace else, toward something mysterious and far away. We try to recapture something that we believe we had years ago in childhood or something that we read about in spiritual books. We try to improve our hunting skills so that we can capture an elusive God, a God who does not want to be found.

But God *is not* missing or elusive or invisible. It is *we* who need to make ourselves ready to receive God, who is always knocking at the door of our hearts, whose Voice is always speaking, whose Heart makes our hearts beat, and whose Breath is the world.

"Receive God." We are the only thing that stands in the way of this ultimate action, this greatest desire, this end point that is also our beginning.

Why do we stand in the way? What you will find on the pages of this book is an exploration of the trail of our resistance to seeing things as they are, which includes the fact that God is always present and accessible to us. It is a step-by-step, sequenced walk through the territory of the human heart, with its great longings and its great limitations. It seeks to show how these limitations— through the grace of God—are always less than the power of the Truth itself. God, Jesus, Amida Buddha, Allah, enlightenment—whatever we call this Calling that calls to us from within our very body and from the world outside ourselves as well, always stands at the crossroads of every moment of life and death, offering us the answers to the great puzzle of being alive.

The Instruction Manual for Receiving God is for everyone. You can be Jewish or Christian, Muslim or Buddhist. You can even be an agnostic or an atheist, because the proof of the holiness of life is in the day-to-day encounters we all have with what is now, what went before, and what will be. It doesn't matter what we call this holiness or what we consider its source to be. It is a felt and real thing.

This book is for all humans who want to become more human. It is for all beings who want to better understand the intrinsic happiness that existence itself offers. To find this intrinsic happiness, we must understand what seems to stand in the way.

Scientists now know that each snowflake is actually a combination of several ice crystals, each formed around a tiny particle of soil. Without their microscopic bits of earth, these celestial creations could not come raining down on us to cover the landscape in quiet and white.

The human ego is like that particle of earth, a condensation of the particular within the great expanse of the universe. It is what the beauty of this world is made from. Without it, the entire journey from separateness to oneness would not be possible. The dynamics of human life would disappear. Seeing and being seen would never arise. Brokenness and healing would never come into being.

The origin of suffering is the existence of the ego, as Buddha said. But this statement is often misunderstood to mean that the ego needs to be eliminated, transcended, or in some way—spiritually or not—discarded. Nothing could be further from the truth.

To be separate, to have a consciousness that rides in a body that begins to grow toward death from the moment it is born—and to know that this is true—is the beginning of the existential suffering all beings share. That—along with poverty, earthquakes, tsunamis, illness, and other tribulations—is part of what it means to be human. Buddha knew this, and he did not mean to say that the disappearance of the ego would cure these troubles.

However, along with these difficulties, we tend to elaborate and improvise. In an effort to secure a completely safe future for ourselves—an impossibility, of course—we actually create additional suffering as we try to stop the world in its tracks, sensing the end of our separate existence at the end of the line.

The human ego—our sense of separateness—is not negative in and of itself. The cause of the additional suffering we all are prey to is the *unhealthy* ego, the ego that *only* knows separateness and that tries to maintain this separateness in the face of a much subtler truth.

However, when the sense of a separate self is understood for what it truly is—God's expression of beauty and the vehicle for the journey home—even the existential suffering becomes more bearable.

This book does not encourage false forays into imaginary worlds where there is no suffering of any sort, where some magical notion of spirit has whitewashed reality into a palatable dollop. Instead, the words in this book seek to awaken you to the truth of God, that perspective and level of integration that allow you to be separate and one with the universe *at the same time*. It seeks to put *life* into perspective and to make our lives something worth living, despite the hardships inherent in the situation in which we find ourselves. In other words, this is a book about *life, now, us,* and *other people*. It is not a book of theory but a set of instructions for living.

Where did you come from but here? Where is "here" but everywhere? What is there to lose, and what is there to gain? We are *creations* and creations are not so much "made by God" as they are God in another form, or God *in* form! Our only job here on this earth is to heal, to return to the wholeness that we already are, having been born from the same milieu from which stars and galaxies emerge.

The human ego is such a star. You are such a star. Your magnitude is tied to your healing, and your healing is always calling to you from your deepest, innermost heart. That is why you are reading these words, why they have attracted you here. If you know this—that your wholeness is always calling out to your wholeness—you are already most of the way home.

This is a book about how to live life with eyes wide open, to see both what you can understand and the unending mystery of existence itself. When our egos are healed, this mystery is not a worthless thing, waiting for a revelation to make it relevant. It is the meaning of life itself. It is its own revelation. It is self-illuminated and always in the presence, the glow, of the Creator.

My hope is that each of these pages heals you. If one page heals you, then this book has done its work. If only one person is healed from this book, then this book has healed a universe.

Life is a journey to see how big our hearts can get. This book is meant to help your heart grow by removing obstacles so that your true intelligence and kindness can flow more easily. This is a book meant to show you that you already have what you need to receive God. You have your own song, and God has a ticket to your concert. If you are shy, God, being God, will sing for you.

Mind, Buddha, God, awakening, liberation: they are all fancy names for being alive and present to what it means to be truly human. I write with gratitude for the hard work you have already put in and for your future hard work. I bow to you. I lift a glass and salute you.

How to Use This Book

In this book, you will find more than one hundred entries that I call *seed passages*, which lay out a real and practical path to making yourself ready to see the reality of God in your life at this very moment. Along with the seed passages, I have written commentaries to open up the main passages and, at times, to suggest a different approach to the idea being presented.

This book is meant to be a chariot, something to hold your body, mind, and spirit as you continue the great journey you have embarked on: the attempt to cure your suffering. It is the fruit of my own journey, from suffering in Brooklyn to joy in New Jersey—not a long distance geographically, but a lifetime of learning, healing, and letting go.

So how to use this book? My first suggestion is to not so much read it as *contemplate* it: Open yourself to those moments when you stop *thinking* about the material and instead begin letting it work on you in its own way. These words will work on you because of where they come from: deep in the heart of what it means to be a human being. So, like a medicine designed to heal the human body, this book, designed to heal the human soul, will seep into every pore of your spiritual self if you let it.

I suggest that you read small sections at a time. One a day or even one a week will do. You can go through the book from front to back or open it randomly. Although there *is* an order and you might find it helpful to follow it, a random choice opens the door to experiencing a miraculous moment of serendipity. Chance is the way God likes to mix and mingle with us, and since God is always present, we always have the possibility of bumping into something that speaks to exactly where we are at that moment, as if someone were keeping an eye out for us.

You can return to passages you want to work on again and again. No effort put into any of these passages will be wasted. As Jesus said, they will all be as "a treasure for you stored up in heaven." Except the heaven I am talking about is right here and now, on this earth and in this life: your life and my life.

You will also find many small exercises throughout: Be sure to try them. But also realize that each seed passage is actually an exercise in "being a new way," in trying on a new perception or point of view so that your life itself becomes your practice.

One of the unique things about this book is the explanation it offers on how to use our suffering—whether it is physical, emotional, or spiritual—to find God, to *receive* God. That is why each of these seed passages is so potent: They all go right to the heart of the matter, which is that God is always there, waiting to be received.

This book is not about creating some grand edifice of theology. It is about the practical steps you can take to actually experience God, and it unfolds in such a way that each step is a complete world in and of itself.

This sounds impossible! Isn't experiencing God—the real Self, Buddha-nature, inherent authenticity—extremely hard? Doesn't it take years and years to achieve? The answer is both "Yes" and "No." "Yes," because in our wonderful creativity, we have succeeded in distorting what it means to be human. This is not exactly our fault. It is part of the journey we take when we step out from the featureless background and become a separate being. This perilous moment is experienced again and again as we "step out" of childhood to become an adolescent, out of adolescence to become a young adult, out of our middle years to become older, and finally, out of our later years to become old. Each step is fraught with difficulty, because we are creatures of habit, blind to what is happening in the present moment, preferring our version of the present to be exactly the same as what went before.

The answer is also "No, it is not hard to receive God." We are all capable of embodying these eternal truths because we are actually *made from* them. These truths are what hold the universe—and you and me—together. Realizing this, we can see freedom in an instant. There is nothing inside us that is not outside us as well. The reverse is also true.

It is my belief that all people can receive God and find liberation, and that this sort of freedom is really what the world is waiting for. It is as if there were hands stretched out at every border in every country on the earth, just waiting for the signal to step forward and grasp the hand of a stranger in love. I know this may sound implausible, but it is true. I can see it in my heart; I can hear the laughter that would ensue; I can smell the delicacies from every country being prepared and passed between hands and people from all over the earth.

It starts with you. It starts with you becoming ready to receive God in your own life—a God who will not damage you in any way; a God who will only love and support you because both you and God are only love.

This book is in your hands. You have already knocked on the door of heaven many, many times. May this book be one of your answers. Make the most of it.

God, human, universe, home. They are all One eventually. My hope is that this book is a beginning for us all.

SEED PASSAGES

When we are consciously, personally aware of who we are—flaws and all, greatness and all—we hear God calling.

How do we find God? We start at the beginning. And what is the beginning? The knowledge that God is always near when wholeness—no matter what it looks like to our egos—is present. "Be who you are" is the great secret of spiritual work.

God receives us just as we are. But we don't receive ourselves in the same way. We don't love ourselves as we are. Our deepest work is not so much to improve ourselves as to realize ourselves, to see ourselves clearly and dearly.

The small self, hearing the words "Be just as you are," immediately takes it as permission to sidestep the spiritual path. It whispers: *Just do what you want! Don't worry! No effort is needed!*

But we arrive at the truly effortless condition only after practice and more practice. The secret here is that we are not practicing being *better* than we are. We are simply practicing *kindness* toward *who* and *what* we are.

Knowing who you are is not a mystical thing but a matter of experience, acceptance, honesty, and compassion. It is knowing you are small and selfish, greedy and angry, great, creative, tenderhearted, and caring.

Imagine for a moment that you are a great Buddha. Because you are a Buddha, you are truly openhearted and not reactive to things around you. You look with compassion on all things because all things—as it says in the beginning of the Torah—*are good.* So the little child stumbling is good. Your heart opens to the old woman grieving for the loss of her husband of many years. You see, with your transcendental sight, that it is good. That being human is good—difficult, but good.

For us to be as Buddhas ourselves, we must leave room for the possibility that our greatness begins to manifest when we can see both sides of who we are—small and greedy, angry and lonely, as well as courageous and tender. Seeing both sides is the openhearted view. It is what allows us to see the world and say, *This too is good.* This is why the Buddha, the Christ, the *Zaddik* all love us. They see that we too are good.

We need only embrace ourselves in conscious awareness, with deep knowledge and without judgment, to feel God.

Reader, stop for a moment.

If you can do this for even one moment, the great Intelligence that is the universe will find you. It is said that God knows when every sparrow falls. But I'll tell you a greater truth still: *God searches for each sparrow, because each sparrow is holy.*

Although we are all born holy and die holy, when we embrace ourselves in the spirit of this seed passage, we light up heaven. God sees the sign, finds us, and brings us home.

■

The personal self is beauty itself—a piece of beautiful God-manifestation turning in the sparkling light, newly fallen on its temporary, tender, and newly existent self.

Many spiritual paths ask us to leave the ego—the sense of a separate, personal self—behind. They ask us to find that place where—they believe—the ego does not exist. But everywhere I look in the universe, from the farthest galaxies to the smallest vibrating strings creating the harmony of the quark and proton, I see the beauty that can only be uttered in the language of separateness. The problem is not in the ego but in the fact that the ego doesn't see itself as the beauty it truly is. Oh, Reader! Let yourself heal into Yourself!

You are God's only child in a universe filled with only children.

In the vast impersonal universe, someone is looking at you.

Though you know somewhere within yourself that you are a temporary thing, soon to vanish in a cloud-chamber trail, someone is looking at you as if you were the most beautiful thing in the world.

This is true for each one of us—if we allow ourselves to know it. *Personal* and *impersonal* disappear as we realize that every created thing deserves and gets this Divine Glance, which is also yours and yours alone. When personal and impersonal disappear, what is left is God's eternal conversation among the stars.

God has never made a mistake in creating individual egos over and over again. We make mistakes in not knowing how to integrate these egos and heal them.

Gratefulness is the heart of a well-lived life. Without gratefulness, our lives have no meaning. With gratefulness, we discover that all the meanings of life come down to this ability to feel grateful. The human ego—when healed—is the best vehicle for feeling this central aspect of our being.

■

It is impossible not to walk to heaven or be pushed toward heaven or be kicked toward heaven while here on this earth.

The great teacher is life itself. Whether or not you have a human teacher, the great teacher is always in session, presenting the greatest lessons in the greatest way.

Of course, we don't always trust life. Life has hurt us. It can be unpredictable, changing course when we least expect—or desire—it. But the more we trust what life brings us on a daily basis, the more the mystery of life reveals itself, until, finally, we are life itself.

■

Awakening is the birthright of every created being. To know God is our destiny.

What would it feel like if you realized that, from the very beginning, you were designed to look for, to find, and to receive God? That you were designed to awaken to reality? How would it feel to know that this would definitely happen in your lifetime, because you were made to accomplish this very thing?

If you let yourself feel this, many things will drop away. Those are the things you no longer need. Try to let them go. What is left is the answer you were looking for and the reason you were born.

■

To be God-realized is to have no free will. To have no free will is to be a completely autonomous being. To have no choice but to be with God gives you endless choices.

We all fear giving up our free will. We think our will—what we want—is *who we are*. We often don't know ourselves except through the medium of this will. But our search for freedom is only complete when we realize that everything we want in our deepest being is what God wants. It is only then that we come to our truest self, the place where there is no conflict between ourselves and God. This is the moment of realization that God is not an authority with whom we engage in some ancient war but is identical with our most essential and tender self. God inside and out, a single, indivisible thing.

You can experience this right now. Say to yourself: *My ego—even with its difficulties—is a beautiful thing, created by God. I need to love it since it is beauty in action. This is God's will for me.* Strangely enough, the more you can say this and mean it, the freer you will be and the more your true self—with its God-connected sense of free will—will shine.

■

Awakening is the moment we become completely human, no longer suffering needlessly and no longer fighting the suffering we must do—and knowing the difference.

One day you realize—or admit—that you are imperfect. It finally sinks in that you are not who you thought you were. You begin to feel terrible about not being perfect. Your self-esteem descends to new lows. Your feelings hover over you like a low-pressure weather system. In addition to feeling imperfect, you now also feel depressed and defeated. You have added one suffering on top of another, depression on top of imperfection, because you have encountered another one of the great obstacles to spiritual work: the difficulty we have with simply suffering and with suffering in a simple way.

Human beings have a tendency to create extra suffering, because we believe the suffering that is part of life—because of life's imperfections—is too much for us to bear. We are unconsciously reminded of our first encounter with this level of suffering: when we were children and could not change our circumstances.

Consider learning to suffer in a new way. As an adult, you can have a different relationship with this fundamental condition of human suffering—a relationship that brings dignity and aliveness. It begins with recognizing that imperfection is a fact of life and that the suffering caused by imperfection will remain, even after we have done all the work we can possibly do on ourselves. It is part of the existential phenomena of being human.

When you can do this, your suffering will help you increase your degree of kindness and forgiveness toward yourself. You will also be kinder to your brothers and sisters who walk this planet in the glory and difficulty of being human. When you do these things, you are truly awakened.

■

Being completely human means we act with kindness—not because we have learned it from a book, but because our nature is kind.

There are two ways to bless food. One is to remember that there is a book somewhere that tells us to bless food. The other way is to be still and simply look at the food before we eat it. "This apple: It's going to be delicious! It was placed in the store by someone. It was shipped there. It was picked from a tree that someone tended." And if that were not enough, somehow there are trees that grow this wonderful fruit, which is just perfect for us to eat! Our bodies love it; our tongues love it. Apples! Applesauce! Apple pie! At this point, you might spontaneously say, "Thank God for apples!" This is the truest blessing, because it comes not only from your heart but from *true seeing*: You see the cause and effect cascading down from seed, to tree, to fruit, to your body. Whenever you see clearly, your true nature stands up and blesses the world.

To be human is to lose our way and find it again. The human lineage is the lineage of falling down and getting up.

Time and again we forget who we are and where we are. We forget God and other people and realization and our true Self. We forget that we are essentially good and connected and at one with the world. This forgetting might be considered a disaster, but if we change our perspective, it needn't be. *To be human is to fall down and get up over and over again.* Please put this definition in your soul's dictionary. And Reader, please join this tribe of the truly human. If you do, you will never be disappointed in yourself again. You will certainly continue to grow and improve, but you will be much less likely to reject your essential and imperfect self—thus tossing yourself out of the human lineage.

To fall is human. To get up again is divine!

Enlightenment doesn't cease to shine because it is imperfect, and imperfection doesn't go away because we are enlightened.

There once were two rabbis who saw God. They heard about each other and agreed to meet. They met in a small tavern in a small village on the outskirts of a small town. The first rabbi, whose name was Mordekhai, looked at the other, whose name was Avraham.

"I have seen God," said Mordekhai, "and my life has changed forever!"

"I too have seen HaShem, our Lord, and my life is changed as well!" answered Avraham.

Mordekhai leaned closer.

"But to tell you the truth, there is something I don't understand. Having seen God, you would think I would be happy all the time, that my cares and woes would be as nothing. But they are not, and I am at a loss to understand why. I have heard that you actually *are* happy all the time. Tell me, what is your secret?"

Avraham waited a moment or two and then said, "Brother. We have both seen God. Of that I am sure. But I have done one thing you have yet to do."

"What is that?" asked Mordechai.

"I have let God see me."

The moral of this story is: The bruised apple is still good for making pies. In other words, *trust in the Creator to see the good that even you yourself cannot see.* Your sorrows do not need to disappear for you to be good in God's eyes. Therefore you need never hide any part of yourself again.

■

The whole program of creation is to bring us back into contact with God.

Why am I here?

Because you want this.

What? This life? This suffering? This distance from the Real?

Yes. Because within you is the eternal program of repair. Do not ever forget that left to your own devices, left to your natural inclinations, your body desires to heal, your mind desires to heal, and your spirit desires to heal. To be broken is the only way to understand wholeness. To be separate is the only way to return to the One. Your whole life is about repair and return. Whether you sit in meditation facing a wall or pray in the sanctuary to God, your soul already knows that all brokenness leads back to home, that "brokenness" and "home" arise together, like sun and sky, like river and water. All of creation was made for this purpose. Everything else is commentary on the search for the eternal.

■

Most of us look in the mirror to see how bad we look. We look for the blemishes, the irregularities: *This is too big. That is too small. This is not the right shape.* But when we look at little animals or little babies, we see them all as beautiful. How could we not be beautiful as well? We don't see our beauty because our vision—our whole physical and psychological capacity to see clearly—has been injured by the early wounds of childhood. If we could see ourselves with Buddha's eyes, with God's eyes, we would see the beautiful creatures we are.

How does Buddha look at you? How does Buddha see you? Imagine this for a moment. His eyes are of what color? His hands in what position? Is he walking toward you or sitting still? Is he smiling? What quality emanates from him as he looks at you?

Now remember: Everything that Buddha is right now—his true compassion and feelings for you as an individual—is not changed because he is seeing *you*. He is not stupid or easily fooled: He sees a being in front of him who is not perfect, who is still selfish, who can occasionally be thoughtless and cruel. And yet he gazes at you with love. Soak it in. Let it fill your heart. His is not a sentimental glance: It looks deep into your soul. It is real and makes you feel more real.

Now that you know what this is like, look at the next person you see with your eyes, which are Buddha's eyes.

Thank God for our defenses, because they have sustained us through the assaults of life and culture.

Our defenses should not be thrown away lightly. They form part of our immune system toward the things that have injured us. In the moment that actual danger appears, defenses are valuable. Every part of our body, mind, and spirit needs a healthy protective system.

The problem with defenses is that they become institutionalized; that is, they continue working when there is really no need for them. When we start looking at the world in a generalized and habitual way, through the lens of our defenses, we see it in terms of what we need to be protected from. Then we lose contact with our true heart, which only exists when we see the moment clearly. The way to see clearly is not to tear our defenses away but to heal them into what they were before they were put to war: the human ability to connect and know what is going on. Defenses are actually a form of intelligence.

"Defenses without the defensiveness" are part of our alert and awake quality. Honor them. Thank them. And then let them rest. Finally, say to God, *Thank you for my defenses, which allowed me to come here, to this day.*

■

Our desire to see God's Light has remained intact, even though we have been hit by boulders, buried under landslides, stoned, and burned. This desire—which is the purpose of life itself—is what our defenses were really defending.

Why do we say we are sorry? Why do we sometimes forgive even grievous injury? What is it about the human soul that can do these things?

Sometimes people denigrate the human desire to be happy, thinking it is a selfish and small thing. But it actually is the ever-present, resilient echo of life that always remains, even in hardship and defeat. The desire to be happy needs to be returned to its true origin: God's voice—Buddha's truth—echoing through our human mind and spirit. Do not be ashamed of this desire. If it has become selfish and small, raise it up. Desire happiness for yourself. And then, if you are truly spiritually adventurous, desire it for all your friends, then all your acquaintances, and then everyone you meet on the street. Keep going. Don't stop.

The creativity with which we have saved our lives is quite touching. But when that energy no longer has to stand guard, it is freed for fresh wonders. Then you are creating in the spirit of God.

In the West especially, we like to link neurosis and genius: "Pain and suffering make great art." But in actuality, pain and suffering make great art less great. Yes, it is a miracle that great creations can still emerge from tortured souls, but the healed soul creates on a level not imagined by the wounded.

Artist or not, this is the same for all of us. Our creativity in keeping ourselves safe, in making a life for ourselves despite the odds, in rising above our painful childhoods is truly touching and amazing. The greatest wonder, however, is what the human spirit can achieve when it is healthy. Then we leave the world of subjective art and enter into the world of objective art. Objective art is the art of living. Objective art creates no schools or divisions: It brings life to all who encounter it. Be an artist of your own soul. Don't be afraid to heal. You will not lose your uniqueness, but instead will gain your true calling.

Let us say that the individual person is a drop of water. Standing beyond this drop is the ocean: the entirety of All That Is. There are no drops of water in the ocean, of course, just water and more water. So there seem to be two worlds: the world of the individual drop and the world of the ocean. It is tempting to think that the single drop is "my individual ego" and the ocean is God. But this is not true. *God in you and you in God is the truth.* It is as if you awoke to find yourself capable of knowing simultaneously that you are a separate bit of water—glistening, wet, fluid, and alive—and that this "drop" was just a moment of separateness in an ocean of water. This ocean is the source of all drops. It makes them and takes them back again forever. It is life unending. Knowing both the drop and the ocean is living the life of the Divine Self. It is one world. One life. One God.

Dear Reader: For the next week—or your entire lifetime, if you are sincere and brave—every time you drink a glass of water, consider it a moment of divinity, a moment when you dissolve into the All and remain exactly who you truly are. This is the true blessing of thirst as it brings us to a moment of awakening.

In true nonduality, we understand that a fish never leaves the water. The fish never comes to the end of the water, even if it is an explorer fish, swimming this way and that. It never comes to the end of the ocean because its nature is to be in the water. The fish and the water are one. As long as we think "*Here* I am whole, and *there* I'm not," we think there is an end to the ocean of self. But truly, there is no end to this ocean.

When we have problems, we imagine a different sort of life where there are no problems and then attempt to get there. Sometimes that works for a while and can even be beneficial, but as a path to true change, it is doomed to failure. *There is no life but this one.* There are not two lives, one better than the other. True change begins with a relationship with what is actually present in the Now.

Try this: Say to yourself, *There is no life but this one.* This doesn't mean that things will remain the same; the nature of life is that things will continue to transform. Nor does it mean you will eternally be caught in the position you find yourself in now. But the subtle acceptance that there is no other life will help you control the unreal, questing mind that is always looking for the end of this world and the start of another. It's as if a bird kept flying at top speed, saying, "Where does the air end?" The bird's nature—its relationship to air—means it will continue to find air everywhere it flies. There is no "bird" without air everywhere! To think—even unconsciously—that there is some life that is separate from our life is fantasy. When we stop our questing in this unreal manner, we enter the place where God helps us change what we need to change and simultaneously be in life as it is. This dance of change and acceptance—which makes up the pith of our lives—takes place in the Present Moment.

Here is an example of the awakened state: I walk into a room where you are in the height of prayer. I call your name, and even though you are in a transcendent state, an exalted condition, you turn and say, "Hello." You still know who you are while being at one with God. That is the state of true grace, and this plainness is its hallmark.

As long as you equate spirituality with some sort of superhuman feat or effort, it will be beyond you. You will never be strong enough or disciplined enough or pure enough to compete with some imagined ideal. Commitment and discipline are indispensable, but they themselves are not the purpose. Their purpose is to stop your habitual mind so you can look at who you truly are, warts and all. When you do that without judgment, you and God will agree that every deep meditation is God calling to you and every distraction is God calling to you again, from the other side of the room.

The secret is that God is not a condition at all. God is *un*conditional; that is, God has no conditions. Grace walks into the room when all the doors of "condition" are open.

Why do we pray? We pray to find happiness; we pray to be in our natural state, no longer separated from ourselves. We are not simply natural people following our natural way. So, in a sense, we pray to try to be natural people.

Dear Reader: Do you know that you are praying right now, reading this? After all, what is prayer really? When you do something that makes you lose your self-consciousness completely, and yet do it with intention and awareness (the difference between the way you feel right now and how you feel watching television), you are praying. Prayer is a natural thing. It is what happens when you are completely interested, and it is this voice that God always hears. Prayer rouses God from his sleep and makes him do holy things.

■

Being a natural man or woman, which is the state we need to be in to be with God, does not mean doing nothing, leaving everything alone, having no bones inside the flesh. It means still having a self, having desire, watching out for things. But it also means being able to melt. We pray because we need to do both—to stand because we have bones and to melt because we are just flesh.

Spiritual work never gets easier. If it does, watch out! Your commitment to doing it may grow, and sitting down to prayer or meditation or exercise may become easier. But just as the graceful, natural effect we see in great artists comes from a commitment to constant practice, so does grace fall on those busy watching the flow of life through the eyes of their particular practice. Practice opens our eyes to the fact that grace is always, naturally, already here.

■

When we are honest with ourselves, God shows up. It is guaranteed. Will that Presence make you jump for joy? Maybe. But maybe that Presence is going to make you cry. Maybe you will weep all night, until your face becomes a thing of beauty, filled with tender light.

What do enlightened or God-centered people look or act like? Are they quiet and content? Do they bow slightly when meeting someone? Is there a mysterious smile that plays around their lips? A special light in their eyes? Here is the secret to finding out how a deeply spiritual person should look: Go to your bathroom or bedroom and look in the mirror. Really. Go and do it now. Maybe the light in your eye is there or not; it doesn't matter. Your "original face"—the one in front of you right now—is the one God always sees. When you see it too, you and God will both be in heaven—and we will get the benefit of you being who you are, here on earth.

■

Imperfection actually turns out to have an element of beauty. The universe has more of one type of matter than another. Things are basically unequal. If this inequality did not exist, we wouldn't have a universe. It is this lopsided falling-into-something that makes beauty; this imperfection itself is the basis of beauty. So the very thing that plagues us— our imperfection—turns out to be a basic element of joy.

No one ever went to a concert to hear a metronome click. (Well, actually, that did happen once, but that concert was never repeated!) Instead, we go to a concert to hear something swing or pulse. The uneven, the eventful, the constantly changing—that is what is in you, dear Reader. Don't be frightened of it. It is the ride of your life.

■

There is a rule that was part of our growing up and is part of our society and part of our incarnated existence, which is: *You shall not know that you are a divine being.* This is forbidden knowledge.

You are a divine being. Do your parents think of you that way? Do your boss or clients? Do *you* think of your parents, boss, friends, or even enemies as divine beings? What does it mean to be a divine being? Does it give you license to do things you would not ordinarily do? Does it make you special? Do you have the right, the divine right, to exert your will over others? To be divine, must you only be small, a servant, or can you also be a king or a queen? And finally, *why* is this knowledge forbidden? Who forbids it? And if it's true, how do you reclaim it?

Here I have given you only questions. But if you think continuously about this and begin to understand it, even a little, I assure you, Eden will resurrect itself right where you are standing, and you will be ready to eat the fruit with God's blessing.

■

Going into the unknown is going into knowledge that is original. Experience that is original cannot be arrived at by comparison, which is where most of our learning comes from, dredged up from memory, contrasting one thing with another.

Our real Self, our true nature, is not found simply by ignoring comparative intelligence but by *using it up*—that is, allowing ourselves to become completely conscious of its secondhand nature. We should not be afraid of our comparative mind—knowledge that really comes from the past. But we must also think and learn about what we really believe and who we really are. The next time you are in the unknown in any way, instead of thinking *I'm lost*—which is knowledge from some other time or place or person—think, *I am free. There are no ideas or concepts that are binding me. Let's see what's here.*

When you go into the unknown, you find yourself in the original sea. It is in this original sea that relationship truly happens.

You are not your father. You are not your mother. You are not your teacher. You are not any concept of yourself from the past. Now: Who are you when you relate to others with this awareness?

■

There is only one safety: the container that is large enough to include existential suffering and ambiguity. The bigger the container, the more qualities of life it holds, the safer we feel.

We were born with the inherent ability to see all of reality, with its contradictions and opposites. When our God is very small, these contradictions and opposites feel dangerous to us. But when God is allowed to be God again—that is, unshackled from the chains of the smallest part of our minds—these same things just make us feel alive. Today, dear Reader, you will encounter many contradictions and opposites: Actively note to yourself that you see these opposites, and enjoy them!

■

The ultimate container is God. That is, a container that holds but does not contain; contains but allows. It is so big, it allows everything.

The God you can hold in your head is too small. Let God fill your body, too. To hold God, you need a universe: When you allow God to enter your body as well as your mind, *you are that universe!*

At the same time, you can be held by God. Only God is big enough to hold all of your contradictions, all of your limitations and difficulties, all of your good and evil. All of you, every part, with nothing left out, is held by God. *Feel this.*

■

If we believe we need to work through all of our neuroses in order to see reality or be with God, we are pretty much lost, because our neuroses and imperfections are endless.

Please, dear Reader, do you think that God or Buddha, Mohammed, Moses, or Jesus needs you to be perfect before you can be with God, before you can awaken or become enlightened? Think for a moment: In your most open state, when your heart is filled with tenderness and compassionate feelings, do you let anyone linger alone outside your door? Don't you open it to everyone, even those who may limp or stutter? Or those whose difficult upbringing has left them with an emotionally distorted view of the world? Of course. You realize that the best way to help is to open the door even wider, to invite the guests in. The same is true for you. God loves you and wants to bring you close. *You, just as you are.* Follow your own heart's intelligent advice: It is not about perfection. It's about your ability to love.

■

Having an "open heart" does not mean being "happy." It does not mean being spiritual or wise or anything at all. It means to have an open attitude toward ourselves.

It is easy to confuse spiritual openness with the personal sensation of the emotion of love, in and around the heart. We are not looking for something so petty! We want action, and the action we want is love-in-action, the extending of the hand of friendship toward our own being. It means not repeating our historical attitudes toward our own faults. It means giving ourselves a second chance, over and over again. It means seeing our true limitations and imperfections, and accepting them with kindness instead of war.

This morning, bow down to yourself. It is not a selfish or egotistical thing to do—you are bowing to your real self, with all its whole and broken pieces.

■

The hard work of truly awakening involves getting a clear idea of just how much of reality we cannot hold, of how much of life we cannot bear. We need to see how limited we really are. Then we will have the chance to meet God in reality and not in the fateful fantasy of saving or punishing ourselves.

The real self is not found in the movies or on the stage. It is not in books and has no script. It is filled with surprise entrances and sometimes inexplicable exits. All of this is OK. It takes practice to let go of some limited idea of perfection or goodness. God is not a reward. God is your own miserable, magnificent self.

■

Learning about and embracing our limitations is the gateway to our true greatness. It is a sort of undressing in the service of truth, a dropping of adornment in order to see the true being adorned in light.

Be naked. You have nothing to lose but pride and fear.

The ego believes that only knowledge and success can bring us into God's Presence, as if God were an achievement, like scaling Everest.

How can the humble find God? The accomplished? The ignorant and the learned? The one of action and the contemplative one? God does not have one way. Only open your heart to yourself, and you will find God's mountain within your own soul.

■

Being with God is a nondual state. This means it can never be achieved by choosing only one side of reality in reaction to a less preferred condition or state.

Words like "God," "awakening," "nondual," and others of their ilk are necessary evils. They open a path to thinking about things, but they block the road, even as they point the way. They make us think there is a special way, a singular way—that being with God or being awakened is a special feeling we need to recapture again and again. But God is kinder than that and makes every place the way home. Every molecule of reality—whether tangible, like matter, or emotional and psychological, like varied states of being—can be a gateway to the nondual experience of God.

Try this: Whatever you are feeling right now has a silent opposite that is present at the same time. So, *confusion* is present with its opposite, *understanding; lost* accompanies *found. Hope* is present with *despair* and *loneliness* with *companionship*, even though there may be no one around to fulfill that function.

Now: Allow both of a pair of opposites to exist. Completely. Vividly. Open your body to this *allowing*. You may notice a subtle feeling of openness, of silence, of expectation without a goal. This is one of the million gateways to God; it comes from being with *what is* in this particular way. Trust this opening, Friend. You can extend it further, to opposites that are more challenging, like *sickness* and *health* and even *life* and *death*. As you do so, the doorway to God will open wider, as wide as your heart.

■

When we realize that we are fully capable of reawakening from our habitual spiritual sleep, over and over again, then even failure, even blindness, is no impediment to being with God.

Spiritual literature is filled with stories of sudden awakenings, powerful experiences that change someone's life forever. But rarely does anyone tell the full story of spiritual awakening. What is usually missing is mention of a relationship with *breakdown, decline, disappointment,* and other words of *dis*illusionment.

Sudden experiences of enlightenment create a tendency to talk about the *perfection of the moment.* This idea is true, of course: This moment *is* perfect. But it is also important to see the brokenness of this moment, of the world, and of ourselves, because these things are the great antidote for the idealization of spiritual states.

God would not be God if what God needed was our perfection. We would not be human if all we learned was to awaken a single time. We need to know that we can awaken over and over again, and that in every state we think we love or hate, in every falling down or rising up, God is with us.

Ecstasy is not something separate from fear. Ecstasy is something that includes fear in the price of being human.

Don't be afraid, my friend,
Of anything for too long a time.
God is in the middle of darkness,
Just as darkness is in the middle of the Divine.

Don't be afraid, my friend,
Be just who you are.
Then the lamp that makes both night and day
Is yours through an infinite time.

■

Ecstasy is chosen.

Choose it: right now! What happened? Did a flash of lightning knock you off the sofa? Did the TV go on by itself? Did God call on the telephone to tell you that you are good?

Chances are that *nothing happened at all.* "Nothing," that is, to our three-dimensional consciousness, which sees only what it can touch in some manner. When we consciously choose ecstasy, all the angels in heaven are awakened at once to help us, to care for us on our journey. But we must remember: Ecstasy is not simply happiness, happiness that is the opposite of *un*happiness. Ecstasy is the condition that arises when both happiness and unhappiness are seen to have a common origin. When that happens, we no longer seek the shallow happiness of light, because we know that the happiness that includes light *and* darkness can never be taken away.

It is the choice of this form of ecstasy that stirs the angels. It is a law of the universe that you receive help with this type of request. *Request. Choosing.* They are the same thing. Do it now and then let go. The rest is up to God.

The graduation to being "truly human" is the culmination of our birthright, the crown of creation. As humans, we are part of the way the universe looks at itself. When we see from this vantage point, we see only other hearts, people on the identical journey to becoming their true selves.

Self-awareness is the final product of the universe. Until the moment self-awareness appears in its full glory, the universe can only see itself partially. When self-awareness—an evolutionary moment in the universe's own plan of growth—appears, we begin to see the possibility of co-creation. That is the moment when we can *consciously align ourselves* with the creative force of the universe, embody it, aid it, and stand by it.

Awakening is another step into self-awareness. It happens when we not only see our separateness, but also see how that separateness is *completely one with the entire universe* and always has been! Awakening is the moment when we consciously align our intention with the force of life, though we see ourselves as small and imperfect. This is the moment we give up seeking to become superhuman and are willing to become *truly human*. Perfection is some marble statue, standing silently in some faraway chamber. To be near God, however, we need to wear a human face— the one we were given in this imperfect world, the one that has the ability to look at itself with love.

■

When we have no territory to defend, God rushes in to where God always was. This is a paradox we understand only as we embrace life fully.

Today, as you go through your usual routine, you will make the choice to defend or let go perhaps ten or twenty times. How can you choose to let go without giving up your own integrity? How can you stand up for yourself and still remain open to all possibilities? The answer is impossible to describe, but the method is clear and easy: Each time you feel as if you need to defend yourself—whether in a conversation with a friend or while making your way through a crowd or by claiming your own place in a line—if you feel you are defending something that is not articulated, that is not named, actually *name it*. Say to yourself, *I am defending MY place in line; MY idea of what should be; MY choice.* When you actually name it, you will be able to let it go more easily. This letting go does not mean you give up your rightful place in either the line or the discussion. It simply means you are not *defending your own existence.* See what that is like today. Perhaps you could choose to do this on every Tuesday or some other specific day. It will become your own, private holy day.

■

Awakening is when we see all the stops on the train line, understand the map of the train line, and feel comfortable inside the train. It is not about some mountaintop. It is about the mountain range and the valley, the earth tectonics and seasons and snows, and how things move and how things change.

What this seed passage is saying is that awakening is not some grand enterprise. It is often presented as such, but that is not its true character. Its true character is a mustard seed. A mustard seed is traditionally considered to be the smallest seed we can see with our eyes. To see the mustard seed level in every thing is to clearly see its essence, its use, and its implications. It is also to continually forgive ourselves when we cannot see these things at all. It is this *clear seeing* and this *forgiveness for not-clear seeing* that become the foundation of our true awakening.

There is a Japanese saying: *The elbow does not bend outward.* It is a smart saying. The freedom of the elbow, the wonderfulness of the elbow, is precisely because of its limitations. This is our awakened attitude. We are free to be completely human. We are not free to be aliens or cartoon creatures. We are free to be ourselves, with all of our imperfections and bruises.

Have you ever repaired a much-loved mug or plate? Once it is pasted together, you might not be able to eat on it or drink from it anymore, but you keep it anyway, on the shelf and in your heart.

Why do we do this? Why do we keep that old sweater or sweatshirt? Those old sneakers? It is because things that are worn and imperfect are dear to our hearts. They somehow have the power to reach through our layers of numbness and touch ... what? There is no name for it. We might, if pressed, call it *the real*. And this *real* has the magical power to make us feel more authentic as well.

Try this: Repair something today. A cup. A sock. A crack in the wall. A friendship. True, it may never be the same as it was before it was wounded, but it might be something better.

To have no identity, we must have a strong identity. It is a paradoxical thing.

Give me your axe. Now, go cut down a tree!

This might be great for some textbook Zen, but it is terrible advice for building a cabin!

The same is true of things of the spirit: To have no ego, we must have a strong ego. That is, to have a healthy ego—one that disappears seamlessly into our entire Self—we must *have* a healthy ego to begin with. Part of spiritual work is to heal our ego into health. Doing that, the ego will disappear into its invisible and true function. We will not hear it sputter or grind its gears. But it will be there, working, bringing us ever closer to God and our own Buddha-nature.

■

The ego likes to think it can achieve a state called "enlightenment," and then its work will be finished. But "awakened" just means you'd better roll up your sleeves and pay attention, because life continues to happen.

Once, in a monastery, when I was younger and in love with enlightenment, I sang as I did the dishes. Now, I sing on stage to other people or to myself in the shower. When I do dishes, I just do dishes (though sometimes I sing when I do them!).

■

Awakening is a continuous process of living and not simply a realization.

There are some people who say, *I had an experience and became enlightened.* It would be far better to say, *I had an enlightening experience.* The first answer brings medals or acclaim or robes. The second answer brings peace.

■

We achieve limitlessness not by denying our body, feelings, or thoughts, but by letting them be, completely as they are, and getting out of the way.

Spiritual integration does not happen by cutting away parts of yourself, even if they are troublesome parts. Unless these parts are given a home they will always come back to haunt you, like a ghost. The great mystery, of course, is how you can gain freedom by allowing something that is limiting you to fully exist in your body, mind, and spirit. You can experience this right now.

Try this: Stop reading and sit for a minute or two, just noting the feelings that are flowing through your body. Some of what you feel may be physical sensations. Or you may experience the play of emotions within your body. In either case, simply let it all be there, exactly as it is, without trying to get rid of it. When the sensations have an emotional content, drop that connection and simply feel them vividly as physical sensations in the present moment. What happens?

The purpose of this exercise is not to quiet the mind but to let the body be as it is, while remaining conscious and aware. This will allow you to glimpse a spacious state in which not only your body, but also your feelings and thoughts, can be brought together to support—and not hinder—your tangible and very real freedom.

■

When you are limitless, your breathing is the breathing of the world. Your thoughts are the world thinking. Your feelings, the world feeling. These activities are not personally owned.

From the point of view of the unhealed personality or ego—that fragmented part of ourselves that does not see the big view—we all need to be constrained in some way. We need laws, inner and outer, to help us do the right thing.

As we heal by accepting all that we are, our behavior will less often be dictated by unconscious internal pressures. Then, outer structure and inner intention will become the same. This is called "taking on the yoke of heaven." It is not a matter of applying more constraint and inhibition. Instead, our natural actions will increasingly become of one piece with what the world and we need.

When the inner and the outer are no longer in conflict, our actions become less self-centered. This allows our interior emotional and mental structures to take in more and more of the reality of other people and the world, and we achieve the long, big view.

You can experience this today: All day long, whenever you have a decision to make, say to yourself, *What would I do if I were completely openhearted and in love with God?* Then, do it.

■

The Heart holds All to itself, making no distinction between manifest and unmanifest, good or evil. At the same time, it is perfectly discriminating, because it is not at all entranced. It is not entranced because the origin of the Heart is not personal but transcendent. The Heart is not a product of history but of Emptiness. Emptiness means "without exception." Therefore, there is no landmark to limit the Heart. When the Heart is Empty, every way is the Way.

The Heart is smart.

We have been created in order to come to God, and we come to God because God is not separate from us in any way. It is God coming to God.

The other night, lying on my side in bed, I felt my heart beating strongly. I thought to myself: *Who set this heart beating? Why does a heart beat at all?* I knew in that instant that "I" had nothing to do with any heart beginning to beat, mine or anyone else's. It's not personal. It's something the universe does for some reason. It creates beating hearts.

This seed passage only makes sense when the personal is not the only viewpoint. To understand it, all you need to do is take a little bit of the personal and push it out of the way. "We have been created in order to come to God . . . " This does not mean there is some "person" standing there, having made us in order to see if we can walk back to him! It means the creation and the Creator are one thing. We could translate this passage and simply say, "Frozen water was meant to become water once again."

Completely true. Simply true. You search for God because God is your origin and your destination. That's what life and death are about: remembering this.

■

The human personality is not a steady, simple thing; it changes from moment to moment. This mutability is disturbing to the homeostasis of the ego.

So we have come this far and have ingested all the truths, and still there is uncertainty and suffering. Why is that? It is because—even as we learn and metabolize the eternal constancies—the one who is searching is the one who is simultaneously resisting this knowledge at every turn. This "resistant one" is the unhealed ego.

The unhealed ego can *never* find the real God, the real Self. It is not that this ego is bad in any way. It simply does not know how to look in the right place. It is the wrong tool for the job. It's like using a sewing needle to garden. It just won't work. But before we can get to the solution, we need to understand the problem: The unhealed ego only feels safe with things that are the way they *were*. It does not feel safe with the unknown, even if that unknown will bring it closer to what it wants: the great mystery of life.

So today, simply get to know the problem. Watch how your ego keeps trying to keep you safe by making the next moment into what went before. Get to know the power that this confusion holds over you. Get to know—without judgment or condemnation—how much it limits your life.

■

All neurosis is an obsession with memory.

"You" are not now. What does this mean? It means that "you" is a concept born of millions of moments of history, from your womb existence to the moment *just before this one.*

In this moment, actually *in it,* there is nothing to be called "you." You don't disappear, of course. But some aspect of your consciousness—the aspect that stands outside the present moment, looks at you through a cloud of conceptions, and comes up with a limited *version* of who you are—is not operating.

What keeps us in the past? We generally call it "the ego." The ego is the part of our body, mind, and spirit that is designed to evaluate, protect, encourage, and inform our being. To do this job well, the ego can't be right in the present moment; it must be in some period of time *before* the present. It needs to gather information from the past and project into the future.

This takes place unconsciously, automatically, and— when no new information can get through—we generate and get locked into repeating patterns. This is what we call a "neurosis." A neurosis is a bad way to lead your life when so much more is available. A neurotic repeating pattern blocks the dawn of each new day. Our job is not to destroy the ego's ability to review the past, but to educate it, inform it, and heal it. The healed ego will always bear the signs of its history, but we will begin to see the difference between living while looking into a rearview mirror and living in the shining of the ever-unfolding present moment.

■

It is the ego's nature to always seek to stop the flow of life and to reflect upon it instead. This brings the ego safety, but also kills what it loves. To put it more precisely, it kills what love *is*.

Love is not sentiment, nor is it a feeling.

Love *brings about* these things, but indirectly. We see the fluttering of leaves as the invisible wind, which belongs to no one, passes through the trees. Love is the wind that makes things happen.

The ego approaches love backward, thinking that sentiment and personal feeling, when brought to fruition— that is, made bigger—will lead to love. It also confuses *eros*, the energy of sexual attraction, with love.

It might be easier to understand what love is if we redefine love as an action. What *actions* of love have you taken today? Actions affect other people and things. Their existence is changed in some way by your use of applied love. Sentiment, on the other hand, only changes you. So today, take any positive feelings you have about a thing (a wall that needs painting or a dish that needs washing) or a person (someone with whom you wish to share a "hello," a get-well card, or a simple smile) and activate it. Doing this is so powerful, it can even halt the ego's attempt to stop the world.

■

Ultimately, healing involves unlearning the patterns that block our natural openheartedness from shining forth. We don't need help to open our hearts. We need help to get out of our own way.

It is winter. Button up your coat! But it is not the coat that keeps you warm; the coat simply holds in the heat of your body. Your ongoing life is the furnace that brings human warmth into the world.

What we have to unlearn is that we need something from the outside in order for us to be worthy. What we have to unlearn is that we need to be a *thing* rather than a walking, breathing, *process*—a flame that lights the world because it is simply being itself.

■

Incarnation into form is itself an anxiety-producing event, because we know the form will eventually change. Nonexistence is an inevitable outcome of existence.

To be born is to be born into trouble. This is not a statement of despair so much as a statement of fact. We need to know this fact in order to live the most enjoyable life. A life built on fiction—such as the idea that we were all born into innocence, or beauty, or a good situation—is not a good life. A good life is built on truth.

This seed passage states a law of the universe: To be in a form, such as a body, is to know instinctively—if unconsciously—that it will change. It will not only change; it will one day disappear. Does this mean you should walk around terrified all the time, obsessed with the existential dilemma of being alive? No. If you recognize the universal truth that some of your anxiety is not *personal* but built into the situation of being alive itself, you will awaken your compassion toward yourself and others.

We are all in the same boat—a small boat on a large and mysterious ocean. This awakened compassion, which can be our constant companion if we choose it, makes life, just as it is, worth living.

■

Unless we can tolerate the universal existential condition of having form, we can't go forward.

The solution to the difficulty of being in a body is to be in a body. What does this mean? Some problems can never be solved, if "solved" means the problem transforms into something else or disappears. Having a form—that is, a body—is very difficult. In fact, whether or not we are conscious of it, most of us are defending against the sensations that run throughout our body most of the time. We do this because these slight variations signal, deeply but unconsciously, the fact that our bodies will inevitably undergo profound changes and even disappear someday.

Having a form means we change. The form itself, the body itself, signals these changes—and their implications—to us. Without accepting the ubiquitous nature of change, we cannot be in the Now. Being in the Now allows us to go forward on our spiritual path. Being in a body while we are in a body, being with our feelings and sensations when we are having them, may not seem like much, but it is actually an advanced moment of spiritual awareness.

■

We can't even approach having a unified experience of life unless we can tolerate being alive, which includes sensations of anxiety about being alive.

Years ago, I had a practice of listening to trees, something I had learned to do when I was younger. I knew that trees had a kind of wisdom I needed to hear. Here is one thing a tree said to me. The words are my own, translated from the language of the tree that I learned to understand: *Trees do not have anxiety. They do not have anxiety because they are rooted and in one place. People have anxiety because they move around.*

I have always remembered this saying, because it is a very kind observation. *People move around.* That is, we cannot avoid anxiety; the existential anxiety of being alive will always be with us—enlightened or not, God-surrendered or not. It is part of our sojourn here on earth and needs to be fully accepted before it will even diminish.

The God we see is the same one the trees see. It is all that is, the dark corners in the roots and the sunlit leaves. Let all of it be part of your tree of life.

The body, when it is accepted fully, resides nowhere. The same is true of feelings. The same is true of thoughts.

This seed passage holds a mystery that I cannot explain. It is something you will have to understand for yourself, as you continue to alternate between the states of contraction and openness that are part of your spiritual path. But I can say this about why we need to experience the truth of this passage: What we call God is another name for a condition that is beyond all conceptions and limitations. It is health itself. When we are healthy, we are *nowhere*, we are *no one*. It is not that we go into some sort of a trance. On the contrary, we *come out of the trance that we are in*. We find that we are not so small as we thought, fitting only in one small body in one small moment. So do not be so automatically afraid of *nothing* and *nowhere*. Before you jump to conclusions, ask yourself: *Do I feel more alive at this moment? Do I feel more free or less free at this moment?* Now I'll say another mysterious thing: At that moment, the answer will come from God.

◼

We think we are only someone. Ultimately, this is an illusion.

My first thought: How small are you? If you think you fit into your body, that is an illusion. How big are you? If you think you are bigger than your body, that is an illusion, too. Only a *someone* can ask these questions. When we cease being a *someone* and are willing to be simple openness itself, then God is our companion.

My second thought: Thinking you are a *someone* is a limiting idea. Not having this idea does not mean forgetting who you are or going crazy. It does mean realizing that most of the elements that you call "you" are ideas given to you by your past history, your parents, and your culture. This is what Jesus meant when he said *a man must leave his parent.* He was talking about having a fresh idea about your true identity. Dear Reader: Step out of illusion by forgetting who you are just a little bit!

■

Out of the many fragrances in the air at a given moment, a bee will be drawn by one particular fragrance toward its source. The bee will come close enough to see the vibrant color of the flower and enter right into the heart from which the odor emanated.

We could say the flower's nectar draws the bee from a world of many things to a world of one thing, from the many smells of the world to the single most important fragrance that resides in the center of the flower. So the flower changes the bee's world.

We must be ready to follow the scent of the nectar that can draw us out of our trance into the heart of our lives.

Think about this: Imagine you are with your child in a mall. Your child is about five. You go into a store, and while you look at clothing, your child strays away from your sight. You suddenly realize this. You run around the store calling your child's name. When you hear no reply, you run into the mall itself, looking in every direction. You are completely concentrated on only one thing: finding your child. You will do anything, enlist any aid, go any distance, make every effort.

The universe is designed to put out the fragrance of truth, and you are designed to detect it. Everything—from beginningless time to this moment—was made for this to happen. One molecule of truth, of true happiness, of true reality, is enough to start the engine in your heart that will make you search for whatever you call God—the Truth, the Real, your true Self. It is also enough for the universe to put all its resources into play to bring you home. *All its resources to bring you home.* Can this be true? Love's inconceivable, unstoppable effort is to find its love: *you.* So never give up. Always have faith. All of creation wants to come to you—and will, if you let it.

■

Awakening is the place where all opposites are held and nothing is discarded. It has complete precision and complete ambiguity. It is clear and unclear.

The biggest obstacle to awakening—that aspect of consciousness that knows it is in God's realm and part of God—is the idea of light and darkness. Our personality's small perspective always has preferences. It wants to move toward what it likes and away from what is painful or difficult. This is only sensible. But in the realm of spiritual work, it is often completely wrong.

The Torah tells us that when God created the world, God said "It is good" at each step of creation. This means that "it is good" was spoken not only at the birth of light, but at the birth of darkness as well. From the nondual perspective of God, light *and* darkness are good and necessary for there to be a created world.

We learn to be like God when we practice holding the opposites of life in a way that returns us to our origin. This does not mean we purposely pursue destructive things. It means that as life comes toward us, it will always come in opposites: happy and sad, safe and unsafe, together and alone.

Your practice for today (or this week, or the rest of your life!) is to simply *notice* the opposites of life as they emerge during your day. The body, mind, and spirit, loving truth, will at some point start enjoying this process. It will bring you ease, pleasure, and—eventually—wisdom.

There is a piece of reality that is intelligently drawing our hearts toward God.

Did you lose faith today? Did you forget that the universe is always calling to you to become whole? To be with God? To receive God, who is always trying to find you?

Dear Reader: Help God find you by saying, "Here I am." *Choosing* to be found by God is the most intelligent thing you can do.

■

All of the strangeness is in the journey. Coming home is completely ordinary.

The saints and robes drop away. The accoutrements of holiness disappear. What we've read in books about what being with God is like is forgotten. We look to our own experience. We worry occasionally that we are not "spiritual" enough. People don't think of us as holy but as "regular," "normal," "nothing special." As we spiritually mature, we find that this ordinariness is our nature. We find that when nothing is holy, everything is holy. It is the ordinary world that is itself the glow of God.

Salvation is the enlightening moment when you begin to have another center of consciousness from which you can view yourself and life. It is more a change in perspective than new knowledge.

Every story about a vision quest or spiritual journey ends with the hero discovering something that was in him or her all along. Our spiritual education is like that: While we discover new things all the time, the deepest things we learn happen when we uncover what was already there. New knowledge changes us; the deepest knowledge *is us*, and we discover ourselves anew when we find it. Trust that everything you need is already within you. Trust your capacity for discovery and change. Trust that the eyes in your head can also see through your heart.

When we awaken, we begin to realize that we are not who we thought we were. We realize that God is present everywhere, which we could call the Great Silence or the Great Transparency.

People talk about God as having no name and no form because that is the most compassionate way they can think of to avoid locking God into a small box. Really, after all, God is nothing much! You can see right through God. God is as transparent as the air between your hand and your face. In fact, God *is* the air between your hand and your face. God is also your hand and your face! So the reason God is invisible to you is that God is the one looking and is what your gaze is looking at.

There is no difference between the material of space and the material of the object: It is all God, hiding there, right in front of your eyes.

■

Think of spiritual practice as a relationship. When practice is *not* a relationship, we think that practice is a "thing" that "we" do. In this way, we forever define ourselves as a "thing" that does some other "thing." *This* thing practices *that* thing! Instead, think of it this way: You *are* practice; practice is *you*.

Instead of the word "practice," we could use the word "prayer." Although we all practice things to get better at them, what does "getting better" mean in the realm of prayer or meditation? Does God or Buddha reward "expert" prayer? And what does expert prayer sound like? The entire question is absurd. The practice of meditation or the practice of prayer is *you as you are*. *You as you are* does not present itself to anything separate from itself but sees itself in the practice. Practice is you; you are practice.

■

Do not do a spiritual practice as if your life depended upon it. Practice as if it *is* your life. Let it be empty. Let it be light. Let it be sweet. Let each moment be a mystery that brings you to the next moment.

"Empty" means *without preconception*. "Without preconception" means you are free to follow the natural course of life. The times you feel the most sweetness in your life are those times that are empty: You look at the baby and feel life is wonderful; you watch the dancer and are glad you are human; you learn something new and are completely satisfied by it in and of itself.

Our greatest spiritual practice is not yoga or prayer or meditation. It is life itself. And how we practice life tells us all. If you practice life in order to someday get good enough at it "to *really* live," then you separate yourself from life in a profound way. But if your definition of "life" is that it has waves of up and down, joy and hardship, ease and discomfort, and if each day you practice being empty of preconceptions, ready to see what life brings, then you will be worthy of the concert stage. The instrument will be your own body, mind, and spirit. The audience will be all the Buddhas and ordinary people who enjoy watching humans be themselves.

■

God cannot be known secondhand.

In Kabbalah, there is something called "knowledge" and something else called "wisdom." What is the difference between the two? Knowledge, which is an important and great thing, can be taught and learned. Wisdom, on the other hand, can be neither taught nor learned. It cannot be taught, because wisdom is the culmination of experience, and experience is internal and personal. Being internal, it has a different texture and tone from things we learn from the outside. It cannot be learned, because wisdom is never a habit and can never be duplicated. It is always fresh, alive, edgy with the friction between mortality and eternity. *Hurry up!* yells wisdom. And when it has your attention, it says, *Be still.* We could also say: *God comes from the heart and not from a book. You must think God up for yourself.*

■

This life may be a mystery, but it is a mystery of love. We simply need to know how to surrender to whatever God gives us, like manna, each day.

One day, I realized that something that had always plagued me in meditation was my own voice speaking to me from the far reaches of my childhood, sending me a message from past times in the only way it knew how. Even though I had thought it was a negative voice, I realized it was not speaking doom or sending out a challenge: It was offering an opportunity to heal a split that kept me from some of the most precious aspects of life. On that day, I discovered that this voice that "afflicted me" was actually my greatest friend.

We may never *completely* understand the fullest extent of God's love and how it manifests in unexpected ways, sometimes within difficult circumstances or impossible situations. But we can make a start by *acting* as if we understand, by changing our behavior.

Do this: Each day pick one small difficulty and hold it gently, with the understanding that something inside this difficulty is precious. Don't demand that God show you the ultimate meaning of this difficulty, but take it on faith: There is honey in the rock.

■

Because we are humans and not ideal beings, we often lose our way. When we take our life as it is, not as some idealized version of who we are or where we should be in our development, God enters. Being in the here and now, we find our true location, which *is* our real Self, our connection to the Divine.

Story after story of human awakening, or "surrendering to the light of God," involves people falling to their knees, either physically or metaphorically. What does "falling to one's knees" actually mean? Whether you are coming from the perspective of Alcoholics Anonymous, Zen, Judaism, Christianity, Islam, Advaita, Buddhism, or any other discipline, when you fall to your knees, it means you have nowhere else to go. It means you have arrived *here* and *now*. All spiritual work is giving up the idealized self and arriving where you already are: not some place *special* or *new*, but here, *where you already are.*

When we are on our knees, we realize we have nothing left to lose—all the tricks we've tried have failed, the strategies have all wasted away into nothingness, we are left empty-handed.

Your hands need to be empty in order to receive. You need to fall on your knees in order to stand up into your authentic and true Self. Try it. You can actually practice being on your knees, either metaphorically or physically, and see what it feels like to say, *Here I am, with no place left to go except to be right here.*

■

The body *is* enlightenment.

The idea of self-improvement has reached a fevered pitch in our culture. But self-improvement is not the panacea for every ill. Some things can only be achieved by letting go of self-improvement and opening to the culture of the imperfect.

Most of us are finely attuned to the imperfections of our bodies, how they fall short of our ideal in some way. But consider the concept of *soma* as enunciated by such teachers as Dogen Zenji and Thomas Hanna. Soma is the body from the *inside*. Not our mental picture of it—which comes from our ability to use our intelligence to compare one thing (our body) with something else (everyone else's body)—but the body from *completely inside*. When we are completely inside our own body, whether in meditation or walking around, a wonderful thing happens: *We become the meaning of the universe, the meaning of life we have always been searching for.* The body is enlightenment, and even in its imperfect, disappearing nature, it is all of life.

■

The ego is a comedian: tragic but true! But when we come to know it's all an act, we can finally begin to laugh.

I completely understand why the spiritual path is described as being difficult. But after all is said and done, it is somewhat of a joke. *This thing that is looking is the problem!* It is never separate from reality or God, but it thinks it is. Simply knowing this, however, is not enough.

Part of the spiritual path is using up the material of this thing we call "the seeker." We must actually spend the currency of our ego until it is poor enough to go on welfare, as it were. When the ego is empty, silent, without more treasure to spend, without more intelligent schemes to promote or try out, what is left is God—right there, within the poverty of our ego itself. God is not hidden, except when blocked by the shadow of the small self that believes it is a mountain. When we use up the ego, it remains as it always was, simply a part of us. The only difference is that we are looking at the sun and not the shadows cast by the small self.

When we have an openhearted attitude toward ourselves, we work with everything that comes—from insight to resistance, from boredom to enthusiasm, from tears to laughter. We are in the arms of the Great Mother who is all things, who accepts all things, and who moves all things toward completion.

The final insight of Buddhism is to be tenderhearted.
The final insight of Christianity is to be tenderhearted.
The final insight of Islam, of Judaism, of life itself is to be tenderhearted.

In the beginning of our search, we think we have to *add* this quality to who we are. At the end of the search, we come to the conclusion that *we are this quality*. Remember, dear Reader: *You are this quality, whether you feel it or not.* Being tenderhearted is like having a nose: It is for other people to see!

■

Have compassion for your ego. It is doing two important jobs at once, which often puts it in agonizing conflict with itself. The ego's first job is to maintain the integrity of the individual, personal self. It simultaneously has the job of seeking out the larger view in which the personal self is only a part. Both are needed.

God needs knees.

Knees need God.

On one hand, we must sincerely ask for what we want. On the other hand, we must express gratefulness for what is already there, with no thought that God is not already present, with no thought that there is something we do not have. This is the proper way to talk to God: hungry gratefulness. Reader! Please have compassion for your poor ego doing so much sincere work!

■

True spiritual growth is impossible without a healthy ego. The ego arises as a natural consequence of incarnation. In other words, coming into being created the sense of a separate self. The ego is not a mutation, error, or anomaly that needs to be eliminated. Instead, the ego needs to be healed in order to take its rightful place in our lives.

Spiritual mistranslation and misinterpretation; partial views; incomplete understanding and poor communication: These things often stand between us and the light. The end point of spiritual study is to trust life. Life contains the experience of being alive and of dying, hardship and pleasure, loneliness and relationship. There is no reason to make believe the ego is something bad that one must "overcome," "transcend," or "get beyond" in some way in order to be a good spiritual student. The simple truth is that the ego, as much a part of our body, mind, and spirit as are our hands and eyes, needs to be healed.

Life itself is the great revealer. To reveal means to "lay bare." It is to find the truth that is already there. Here is a truth: You are a being who has an ego. When the ego is unhealthy, it can be a troublesome thing—so pay attention to it, listen to what it is trying to say. Then get teachers for it, kind teachers who know the route from the past (where the unhealed ego lives) to the present moment (the place of the ego's healing). In the present moment, there is no separate ego; there is only the helpful presence, in the same wagon, riding home.

The Self is the state of being attained when all aspects of the body, mind, and spirit are present. This Self appears not when we conquer suffering, but when we have a true connection to the basic imperfection of our human condition.

The house assembles itself. Of course, this is not our usual understanding. Our usual understanding is that *we build the house*. This is also true, but this second truth should not block the truth of this first principle: Reality likes to make itself. This is what Jesus was talking about when he said, *Consider the lilies of the field ...* Why should we consider them? Because, left to their own impeccable plan, these lilies express completion and delight. *Consider the lilies of the field, how they grow; they toil not, neither do they spin. And yet I say unto you that even Solomon in all his glory was not arrayed like one of these.*

If earth were missing, the lilies could not manifest their beauty. If sunlight were missing, again, no beauty. If any piece were missing, this mysterious thing called "wholeness" (which Jesus called "lilies") would logically not be there. Even the winter frost, so harsh and deep, helps the lilies quicken in the earth on their way to the day they arise in beauty.

All of ourselves must be consciously allowed to exist for our wholeness to be born. Reader: Don't be afraid. Make room inside yourself for who you are. Start with a small grief and allow it to find a home in your heart. Then try another and yet another. Eventually, sensing the sweet nectar that arises from the presence of what you have been keeping hidden, you will take on bigger and bigger tasks, until all of life and death will be yours to play in. This is what is meant by *at play in the fields of the Lord*. That is what lilies do, out there in the glorious light.

The Self is not something that is attained, but something that appears when we give up trying to attain.

Our small self has a million reasons to keep chugging along in its desire to "get better." Improvement is the only way it knows. It imagines that it will get to its final goal of "being with God"—more correctly stated as "getting out of pain"—by getting better and better. But the ladder of improvement must at some point give way to the last step, which cannot be negotiated by the further movement of climbing. This rung teaches us that though the ego will eternally want to improve, improvement itself will not bring us to God. This is an important moment. It can lead to a level of acceptance of the personal self that is so profound it even includes the ego's continual desire to "improve." Self-improvement is not a problem when it is seen as just one aspect of life. The last step on the ladder is to abandon the belief in the ladder as the only road to heaven.

■

What is Sabbath? It is a day when we rest from creating illusions. When we have Sabbath in our souls, we are plain. When we are plain, we are with God.

On Sabbath, it is a Jewish tradition to light candles. Is one person's lighting superior in some way to another person's? Perhaps outwardly this might be so: There's no end to stories about totally focused beings whose every action glowed with holiness. What a thing it must have been to share candle-lighting with them!

On the other hand, I might prefer something less dramatic, some "plain" form of candle-lighting that could take me from a place of conceptualization (candle-lighting as power; spirituality as power; intention as power) to a wordless simplicity.

The fact is, if you just do any action so straightforwardly that you are fully engrossed in it, that is enough. Being with God, enlightenment, awakening—however we define what we yearn for—is ultimately not our concern. In the beginning, we may long for it, live for it, and even die for it. But a sign of spiritual maturity is that we give up all that. We light the tapers, knowing only later that it was our own soul that was burning.

There is no form of freedom that does not include our limitations and suffering.

Do you want to eat something delicious? Then eat the whole apple. If you eat only the core, you are foolish. If you eat the skin alone, you will go hungry. If you peel the apple, exposing its inner fruit with no obstacle to your teeth, you will miss the crisp snap that is also part of the experience of eating an apple.

My advice? Let God taste all of you. Don't be ashamed that you have a fruitless core, a hard skin, and a soft pulp that turns brown in its unprotected state. If you let God eat you up completely, God will be your constant companion. Yum!

■

The most lasting revelations are the ones that were somehow always known but *unthought*. The return of this information to the light of consciousness comprises a level of revelation that can be instantly integrated into daily life.

Being a spiritual seeker will not keep you from death. There is nothing that will save you. Now, you know this already, correct? Yet you do not like to think about it. Known but unthought.

Dear Reader: If you want to *use* death instead of letting death use you, you must begin to think all the unthinkable things you already know but do not let yourself utter to your conscious mind. When you start to think these thoughts, they will break every chain you yourself have put in place.

■

The aim of receiving God is to become more human, not to arrive at some transcendent state in which the difficulties of being human are not present.

How my ego longs for ease! And what is ease to the ego? The absence of everything that makes up my humanity. My ego wants no fear of death. It wants to be clear and composed all the time. To be *incredibly* kind. To be wise in every situation. To be honored but never to get a swelled head. To be loved.

My real Self longs for ease too. However, it knows I can experience freedom from the fear of death only by accepting the fear of death. It knows I cannot always be composed and clear, and it does not demand that of me: It only wants my humanness. And pride? And the desire to be adored? These too must be held close in the light of consciousness; otherwise they will go on their merry way, underground, causing quiet but persistent mayhem!

It is so hard for us to give up our quest for perfection. To be who we are. For this reason, I've invented a new name for God: "The One Who Helps Us Give Up." Call upon this God. Give up illusion for the real thing.

■

The ego personality, even while completely desiring and longing for freedom, resists moving toward it, because it fears its own annihilation.

Dear Reader: Do you sometimes feel like no matter how hard you try, you do not make the sort of progress you would like on your spiritual path? Why is that? Do you lack something? Some genius for change? Were you wounded too deeply in childhood to receive your life's dream, to be with God, to awaken?

Please note: There is an active force that holds you back! The same part of you that searches also looks longingly backward toward your own imprisonment. This is not a theory. It is a fact. Everything that lives has a force within it that makes it want to keep on living in the same way it has always lived. Your small self fears this new, unknown land you are trying to enter and actively seeks sanctuary in limitation—the very limitation you are trying to escape!

So don't escape. Stop trying so hard. Open your mind and heart to this part that cannot go forward and cannot go back. See its dilemma. If you do that, you will begin to notice a form of spiritual progress you never dreamed about. You will begin to come alive.

■

The purpose of all physical manifestation is to untie the knots that keep us separate.

The path of the spirit is filled with paradox: We exist in a limited, temporary form, and from that form we try to see eternity. Yet the secret within the secret is that every existent thing is saying *Hosanna*. This Hosanna is not aimed at anything; it is just spoken, the way the wind just blows because it is the nature of the wind to blow. To praise and bless is the deepest nature of all things in this manifest world.

How can you get to this state? Love your body's sensations: all its quirks and aches and blocks and movements; its feelings, its textures, its hot and its cold. If you do this, you will begin to untie yourself. The cords around your heart will fall away. You will see that you are your own gift, the one you have been waiting for!

■

Once we sense and know God's Presence here, this world becomes something holy, and we become something holy—something we already are.

This seed passage also works in reverse. Start with: *You are already holy* and watch the world become holy. Everywhere you look, you will see the glow of rightness, of being in the right place at the right time. If you continue this for a whole day, you will end up at the beginning of this seed passage: *Know God's Presence here.* This is a good thing.

■

God is also in the condition of separateness itself, lest we think that God could be absent in *any* realm.

Some teachings talk about "the absolute" and "the relative," as if they were two different things. This is a mistake. More properly, we should talk about the "oneness of Oneness" and the "oneness of Two-ness." If we translate this statement into theistic language, it means that God's love really does stretch from one end of the universe to the other, that this Presence—also called Love—exists not in some special state that reconfigures this world of duality into something more spiritual, but actually *is* duality itself!

Let us translate again: This world, with its pain, its serious anguish, and even its unfairness, is also filled with benevolence. You need not go anywhere but here. The more you are here, the more you are within God and God is within you.

■

We must finally find that God does not leave us even when we are convinced that God is not here.

A pocket is made of emptiness. It is useful to hold all sorts of things. Do you dare call this pocket useless because you cannot see the emptiness? In the same way, the Emptiness of God is what makes you possible. It is what allows you to exist. I'm glad you are here with me, in this Emptiness of God.

■

The healed human personality appears not when we achieve perfection, but when we encounter the all-pervasiveness of God, the state of Constant Presence that does not come or go.

God's Presence comes and goes as long as we think something can stop it from flowing. For many people, this something is grief: "If there is grief, there is no God." For others, it may be sadness or depression or anger or despair. For still others, God may disappear when there is no peak experience on the horizon, when things are plain, when there are no mountains.

We could say that God is absent when we *think* God is absent. In other words, *thought*, our thinking, is the only thing that stands between this bright sun and us, casting the shadow of "God is not here." This means we must work with our thinking in a new way. This is what meditation is for, what prayer is for: to go beyond thought until thoughts are like clouds whose shadows float on a moving river.

When we go beyond thought, we realize that *we are the river* and that anything that seems to stand in the way is simply a passing shadow which has substance only because we believe—and think—it does.

■

Even in the light of God, the individual personality does not disappear. It is not unimportant nor should it be regarded as an illusion.

You are walking along a hillside toward the sea. The scrub is moist in many places, and the green and brown brush waves slightly in the wind. Suddenly you spy a speck of vivid color: It is a wild iris—small, intensely purple, beautiful.

If we think that surrendering to God or living an enlightened life is in some way colorless, we need to think again. All of nature is enlightenment in action. It has its own teaching for us. It is the manifest Presence of God. Autumn leaves. White snow. Blue sky. Deep, dark night—it is all beautiful.

The ego is God's version of human beauty. It does not disappear when it is healed and takes its rightful place within the body, mind, and spirit of a human being. The healed ego is our truest, most benign, and beautiful human self. The unhealed ego—self-centered, anxious, alone, and afraid—is the illusion.

■

The human personality, shining brilliantly forth, is seen as a creation of God: the operative vehicle of joyous service to the Truth, which is called Divine Pleasure.

The word "ambiguous" is usually used to mean *uncertain, hazy*, and *unclear*. But it has a deeply spiritual meaning: *having more than one view; having more than one possible meaning*. Pleasure, like childhood play, is ambiguous. This means it is not only about one thing or another, like some task or job, but is a shifting continuity, a continuum of all states. It morphs, first this way and then that, as it fills the available space with a constantly creative flow, ever-changing in dimension and intent, supremely good and alive.

Is this not a good description of the real Self? Of God?

Dear Reader: This sense of Divine Pleasure, which is very close to the ambiguous play of childhood, is within you right now. Ask it out on a date. Coax it from its hiding place, deep within the cave of your adulthood. Let it see the light of a new day.

■

Joy is the result of openhearted acceptance of the inevitability of personal suffering. It becomes an option as we grow into our true fate.

"Our true fate." When we are in a bad mood, we think our true fate is to grow old and die. But what truly is our fate?

Try this: Close your eyes. Watch yourself breathe without trying to change your breath in any way. Accept it as it is. After a few moments, ask yourself, *What is my true fate?* You may feel a moment of sadness arise. Don't be alarmed and don't interpret. This is simply the first gate: sadness.

Now, consciously refrain from interpreting this sadness as some sadness from your past. If you have been brave enough to do this, you will notice that your new sadness has a tenderhearted quality. This is the second gate.

Contemplate that tender feeling for a few moments. If you look carefully, you will notice that there is a new aura around this sadness: It is a quiet joy. This is the third gate. You may never have known this quiet, small joy before. Just be there and watch yourself grow into your true fate.

This universe is set up so that everything that we can be in the presence of, and remain whole with, returns us from dust to diamonds, returns us to our inherent wholeness.

Words like "forbearance," "patience," "faith," and "trust" are attempts to get to the truth of this seed passage. However, none of these words actually explains what this truth— which is another fundamental law of life—really is.

Growth happens in two manners: in quantities, which we could call stages, and in qualities. When we are children growing into adulthood, we could be said to be growing in stages, one stage moving into another in a continuous manner. However, it is also true that each stage has a completely different *quality*: We change in some essential manner. Our world view, our consciousness itself, is completely different from what it was in the previous stage. So it is not just a matter of "more of the same, only bigger." It is an entirely new quality. Change is continuous and discontinuous at the same time.

Continuous change happens naturally: Life goes on, and whether we change in consciousness or not, we get bigger. But we don't necessarily outgrow the younger stages of life. As we know, there are many people walking around—including ourselves at various moments—who are essentially babies in grown-up clothing. To change *quality*, however, we must be able to get to the point where what shattered our consciousness in one setting no longer has that power.

For example, you arrive home at your parents' house. Mom and Dad do something that just drives you crazy. Before you know it, you are in the same old argument. This is example one. Example two: You arrive home. Mom and Dad launch into the same old behavior, and you think, *There they go again. They can't help themselves.* In the second case, you are not affected. You have worked through the identification with your parents and the acceptance of yourself as a separate being. You no longer shatter in the face of that particular storm. You have experienced not only *continuous growth*—that is, having grown older—but also *discontinuous growth*. Your quality has changed. You have returned to yourself.

All of spiritual growth is about this change of state, from one quality to another. When you are a person of quality, you can be said to be a person whose consciousness is whole enough to linger in more of reality longer. Reality—God, transcendence, awakening, and so on—is the ability to let all the proper qualities live in each particular stage of your life.

■

When every pain, every separation, is allowed to exist in fullness, the Light it is made of begins to emerge. It is the radiance of something freshly watered, the shine of what it is, which of course, is God.

Question: What is the Light of this world made of?

Answer: This world itself.

There is no special quality added to this world to make it holy. Yet, at moments, we all see a holy radiance within which everything in the world is fine: Life and death are fine; irritation and failure are fine; love and success, finding and losing are all fine. *The world shows its true colors when we show our true colors. We show our truest self when we allow ourselves to be filled with who we are—pain, difficulty, and all.*

Today, be a Zen master. If someone asks you how you are, don't smile benignly or bow, looking mysterious and cosmic. Instead say, in a full and rich voice, *I'm dealing with my suffering! There's no where else to go! It's wonderful!* Don't say it too loud; however, you might start gathering disciples!

Our preference for either unity or duality—God or God's creation—interferes with our capacity to see all of God's truest kindness toward us.

What is most astounding about kindness is its combination of a precise understanding of what is going on—in other words, its intelligence—combined with its ability to turn the other way, to accept the situation as it is, to receive the whole, with its fractures and pain, in a state of true acceptance.

The other day I heard someone say she could forgive but she could not forget. On the surface, that sounds like intelligence. But the person who spoke had not been transformed by kindness. And the person she forgave had not been transformed either. To be kind, we need to understand exactly what we are going to forgive . . . and then, we need to forgive.

Both head and heart are the required ingredients for the nondual elixir known variously as compassion, kindness, and openheartedness. When these ingredients are combined in proper measure, the result is transformation for all. It is the way God's mercy operates in this world. Then its blessing falls, as Shakespeare said, equally on the giver and the receiver.

God has placed the whole in each piece of the world, and everything that is, is holy.

It is proof of God's infinite mercy that this world—no matter how lost it often seems—is really the million, million gates to heaven.

Although we all go to special places and do special things to put us in the mood to experience God, God does not reside in any one place to the exclusion of all others. There is no one prayer, no one ritual, no one personage, no one saint, no one scripture. Instead, because God is wide and wise, every bit of this world—every atom and curve, every piece of light and darkness, every aspect of death and life, every human utterance, every sound of high mountain thunder—is really a portal to the unification of heaven and earth. If we understand this, we can find a doorway home in every direction we turn.

Everything that is, is holy. Try out this formula today. Remind yourself of it over and over again. Use it even with things you do not understand or do not like. Instead of making you powerless, willing to accept the status quo, it will make you powerful. Seeing the holiness in everything makes you holy. Being holy, you return to your home among all the holy things of this world. This is your true nature and your ultimate fate.

■

There is no place devoid of God. God stands at the bottom of our soul. God *is* our soul. God is the very reason we exist. Our real Self is nothing but who we are.

If you think you are made of stone and live in a world of water, you are going to feel isolated and without hope. You will feel that you do not speak the language of this water world. You will feel alien, removed.

If you think you are water in a world of water, the world will open to you. It will flower before your eyes. *You*—what you take for "yourself"—will flower as well. You will feel opened wide. Your heart will sing.

Part of the spiritual path is beginning to understand that we are made of the same material and of the same spirit as this world. God is looking for God. When we really feel this, nothing separates us from our glory. The world to come—that world of faraway heaven—and this world, which seemed devoid of light, become the same thing.

Now is not only a time: it is a place.

The mysterious Now! So close, we are sometimes told, we cannot see it. So transparent, we are often told, we are looking in the wrong place. Either we are told it takes years to get there, or, if we were smart enough, we would see that we are already there! In any of these cases, it's a sad affair: We end up feeling that there is no real clue to lead us home to this Shangri-la of time, the Now.

But there *is* a map to the Now, and it is easy to read: Simply pay attention to where you are at all times. If you stop thinking of "where you are" as a way to *get someplace else*, and instead think of it as Here, you will automatically be in the Now. Here and Now exist together. They are never apart. So remember, dear Reader, when you want to be in the Now, be Here! Use your body to guide you to Here. To be in one place at one time is to be in your true location. To be in this true location is to be in the heart of God.

Whether you are conscious of it or not, life is intrinsically whole.

Life has many problems. We could make a list:

Life is unfair.

Life is confusing.

Life is painful.

Life is too short.

But please do not add to this true and penetrating list of life's problems the idea that life is not of one piece, that life is not whole. If you can hold in your mind the truth that *life is whole* at exactly the same time that you recognize the validity of the list of life's problems, life will suddenly seem much more manageable and alive.

This is a mysterious thing—that life should contain all of life's problems as part of its wholeness. We have trouble understanding this wholeness because we look at life with a part of ourselves that stands apart, as if we were not part of life, but only an observer of life. But this part that stands and looks, it is life, too. The problems we see so clearly are part of life as well.

Please begin to think of life as a single thing, not as a collection of "parts" and "pieces." Life is not the sum of its parts: *Life is a single thing.* Thinking of life this way will change you. It will not stop you from trying to improve life. It will just show you that "improving life" is part of life itself as well!

Dear Reader: What you have read is true. When you make this truth your own, by seeing that *life is whole* at every moment, you will immediately start growing into wisdom.

∎

Going into the unknown is the Self. Refusing to go into the unknown is the Self. Saying "Yes" is the Self; saying "No" is the Self.

What can you do to escape reality? Nothing. What can you do to escape God? Nothing. Both questions are like asking a fish to swim to the end of the ocean. Just as a fish's nature is endless water, our nature is to *be,* in all the ways a human can be. Nothing we are or can be can take us out of the ocean of our humanity.

The difference between a God-inspired being and a God-forgetting being is this: When your life is centered in the ocean that has no beginning or end—because *it is identical with who you are*—that is, when you understand that your nature is endlessly divine—you are awake. Otherwise, you are asleep, dreaming of wholeness, searching endlessly for an ocean you think you lost or from which you were exiled long ago.

When we can experience our human hopes and fears, our joys and pains, free of their historical issues, we enter what is called the nondual perspective. Here we come closer to living a truly human life—human and limited, yet free.

What does it mean to be limited? It means we have a use. A hammer is not a screwdriver. It is limited to hitting things and not turning things. Its limitations and its usefulness are interconnected: They arise at the same time.

Usually we experience our limitations as something painful, as proof that we are not good enough. But we can return our limitations to their usefulness by separating them from our historical pain—that is, we can allow these same limitations to enter into the present moment, just as they are, without resonating with our past experiences or actions.

If you stop digging up old memories and comparing what you are with what you were, you will find that you and the world will come into focus at the same time. Your limitation will show itself as part of your glory, part of your unique usefulness to the world. This is the type of individuality that does not set you apart and yet keeps your human uniqueness intact. Then you are limited *and* free, no longer at war with yourself.

■

The freedom of being with God or living from within the real Self is ultimately the ability to be simply and fully human.

Dear Reader: Please cast aside all the stories you have heard about saints, perfect masters, miraculous priests, sage-like rabbis, white knights, heroes, and superheroes. We are not interested in paintings, storybooks, television shows, glamorous movies, or other fiction. We are interested in human beings.

The hardest job in the world is to be simply and fully human. This does not mean to roll along, acting out all your insecurities, uncertainties, and partial selves. It means to constantly be kind to your poor, unevenly developed, incomplete, and sometimes confused self. This addition of "kindness toward the incomplete" is what makes you completely human. It gives you the context in which you can exist in wholeness. This kindness-toward-the-incomplete is God's gift to you. It is the actual Presence of God in you. It is the way God finds perfection in this incomplete and imperfect world.

The Self is always present in equal measure in each being.

There are people who can sing and people who cannot sing. But *music*, that universal force, is present in every human being. We are made of rhythm. Whether we like classical music, rock, or jazz, or even if we never listen to music at all, our heart beats to it, our intestines move to it, our cells communicate to each other using it. We don't need to know this is true in order for it to be true. It is simply built into the reality of existence.

In the same way, no one person has any more "Self" than another. It is the paradox of God: *Every bit of God is present in every place.* God cannot be located or limited to one place as opposed to another. God is not a resource that one place or person has more of than another. And although one place may put us in the mood to find our connection with God more than another place does, that is only about our mood and what we need to get there. Once there, we all enter the same ocean. It is the same size for all: *infinite.*

Take a moment to purposely think about several other people and say to yourself, *All of God is present in them right now, and all of God is present in me right now.* In this way, you will stop thinking of God as a commodity, as a value that a person can have more or less of. Instead, you will begin to have a body-centered notion of what the infinity of God is like and how this infinity can fit into one small human body.

■

"Who are you?" is the question that brings you to the Absolute. "You" is the answer that returns you to the world.

Out of the black moist earth comes a small shoot, a young green plant. This earth was made to grow such a being. In fact, this moist cradle is humus—earth made of plants that came before, lived, and then died to make a home for new plants.

The particulars of the world emerge because the Absolute, the Unchanging, sets the stage for all of creation to come into being. It is its very lack of characteristics, its complete openness, that creates the space for everything to appear. The essence of creation is separateness and constant change: Everything is born, lives, and dies. God is the whole thing—the changeless ocean that allows the world to come into being and all the separate waves, the living and dying pieces of this world.

We are a natural, inevitable consequence of the unchanging nature of the Divine. It is not a mistake that we are here. We are the Unchanging's delight. You might say that we are the book that God reads and God is the story we tell.

■

In God, all is one and all is separate simultaneously. In receiving God, we are one and separate simultaneously.

Every culture has an ideal hero. In the West, it is the individual, the man or woman who stands up against all odds, who finds his or her own way. In the East, it is often the one who has gone beyond, who has given up ego and separateness, who devotes his or her life to others.

Dear Reader: Please don't be fooled by cultural images of what a truthful man or woman looks or acts like. I tell you this: *In God, all is one and all are separate at the same time.* How that looks in *you*, how you act when you are filled with this truth in your own original way—well, that will be something worth seeing! I can't wait to meet you on God's Boulevard, where every man or woman of truth eventually finds his or her way.

■

The Self appears when we give up attaining and remain just as we are, in awareness, but not in identification.

Are you a hat when you put one on your head? Did you become a Jew or a Muslim or a Christian the very moment when the naked baby you were came into the world? Please do not get me wrong: I am not talking about whether you were born into a tradition or follow a particular path. All of that is fine. But, dear Reader, please go further! Who were you at that moment, before you were named *this* or *that*? Simply because you did not have a name, or because nothing in you was named, does not mean that you and God did not exist together. In fact, you might have been closer to God then than you have ever been in your life since!

My advice? Be whoever you want to be, follow whatever path you wish, but don't believe in that identity! In fact, if you do whatever you do with complete love, you will find yourself returning to that moment when no name—no matter how small or thin—separated you and God. This is God's true Name, and it is truly yours.

God is present in Presence. God is also present when God is not present. This is the paradox of Constant Presence.

The great end point of human life is death. Because we see life this way—as having an end point—we identify "life" with "consciousness" or "presence." But this is a small understanding of the full spectrum of life.

Let's imagine this for moment: A person who has deeply expressed his or her true nature or, to put it more theistically, has deeply surrendered to God, becomes ill or unconscious. What happens to that person's spiritual understanding? Does it disappear when conscious awareness disappears?

The answer, which is incomprehensible to the small, egoic view of life, is that it does not. God is not limited by "yes" or "no" but is that which makes "yes" *and* "no." The Creator of both day and night is beyond day and night.

Constant Presence is a gift that God gives humanity. It means that whether you are aware of God or your Buddha-nature, it is always present and inconceivably whole. It is never less than completely whole. It means that all opposites are transcended; that human limitations are meaningless in the face of this truth; that God is present in life and in death, not necessarily as that small thing we call "our conscious awareness," but as something so large it includes us completely.

Only poetic language—such as when the Kabbalah speaks of a "lamp of darkness"—can capture this idea. Only you, a small, precious human presence, can embody it. Dear Reader: Please be your own poem. If you do that, you will be one with the universe, as you always were anyway.

■

God is the name of that kindness you find in your heart.

God finds you infinitely kind. Do you believe that? You know your faults, your shortcomings. You know how selfish and small you can be at times. Yet, I assure you, God finds you infinitely kind.

Let me tell you why: You have taken a body. You have come here to hold high and low, good and evil, day and night—all of creation—in one place at one time. You hold it in your body, your mind, and your spirit.

What a magnificent thing to do! You may be entranced by your failures, but God is entranced by your success, your courage, your hard-earned wisdom, the life in you.

When you feel faint at heart, when you get lost in despair, if you lose your way, ask yourself, *Why does God think I am so wonderful? How can this be?*

Send those words up to heaven. Whisper them or cry them out, but send them up to heaven. You will feel the answer because you were made to feel it. It is closer than the agonies we all sometimes feel. It is beneath everything—a bedrock, a sturdy foundation. In the face of this fact of love—a fact that fills Buddha with delight, that fills God with delight—nothing can stand in the way.

You are leaving this book. You are entering your life. They are no different from each other.

Be blessed.

■

Kindness is being with what is.

Right now, what is going on is the holiest of all things.

ABOUT THE AUTHOR

Jason Shulman has been sharing his knowledge of reality and the Divine with spiritual seekers from around the world for over twenty years. One of the foremost exponents of Kabbalah today, he is also the creator of a unique body of work that offers a living experience of the non-dual state.

Born in Brooklyn in 1947, Jason has been passionately involved in exploring the nature of life since earliest childhood. A musician, poet, painter, healer, and spiritual teacher, Jason's original work comes from his commitment to walking the path of being human. His spiritual teachings sit at the confluence of the world's sacred traditions and seamlessly reconcile the theistic approach to God as found in Judaism, with the Buddhist paradigm.

His work has spread internationally through *A Society of Souls*, the school he founded in 1991. Here, he has trained hundreds of students in Integrated Kabbalistic Healing, the Work of Return, Impersonal Movement, and the Magi Process, all of which take a non-dual approach to healing the self, the other and the world.

The first generation of teachers is now sharing the work of this lineage, which is committed to the continuous awakening of humanity for the sake of all beings.

Contacting *A Society of Souls*®

A Society of Souls is a community of people studying and practicing the spiritual and healing work developed by Jason Shulman:

Integrated Kabbalistic Healing®
Impersonal Movement℠
The Work of Return™
The Magi Process℠

You can contact the author or the school through any of the following:

Email: ASOS@societyofsouls.com
Telephone: 908.236.0543
Mail: A Society of Souls
      Box 626
      Lebanon, New Jersey 08833

A Society of Souls web site can be found at:
www.societyofsouls.com